Don't Go

JOHN ELIOT

Illustrations by
Dave Daggers

MOSAÏQUEPRESS

First published in 2016

MOSAÏQUE PRESS
Registered office:
70 Priory Road
Kenilworth, Warwickshire
CV8 1LQ

EDITOR OF THIS COLLECTION: Paola Fornari

ISBN 978-1-906852-36-8

Printed and bound in the UK.

Dedication

This collection is dedicated to my grandchildren,
Cameron, Carlton, Scarlet and Lilwen.

Preface & acknowledgements

Sometimes people ask me what my poems are about. You
can decide. I can tell you a little about their inspiration. I was
a teacher of religion. The reader will find examples of poems
that reflect religion, such as *Prayer*, *John 1* and *Crucifix*. The
bones of Richard III were found in my schoolyard. Richard's
wife, Anne Neville, was married to her first husband in
Angers Cathedral, close to my home in France. There is a
poem in this collection about her. My mother died during
2015. Naturally the death of a person so close to me affected
my poetry, as did the death the same year of two close
friends. I was shocked that they were the same age as me.

I love music. My tastes are broad. I play with words as a
musician such as Miles Davis plays with notes. I believe
the reader can hear this in poems such as *Framed* and
Frame of Words 4.

Poetry has opened new and interesting doors for me.
Since my first collection *Ssh!* was published by Mosaique
Press in 2014, I have been asked to read at a literary festival
in France, and was commissioned to write and read 12
poems at the Musée des Beaux Arts, Angers, France for a
photographic exhibition. My poetry has been translated and
read on French radio. I read regularly in Cardiff at events
such as Megaverse, and was asked to read at Cardiff Central
Library.

There are people I must acknowledge. It is difficult in a
few words to express my gratitude to my good friend, editor
and proof-reader Paola Fornari. She has understood my

poems and helped me take them to a higher level. My
thanks also go to Dave Daggers for his illustrations, with
special thanks to Gill Krnjulac for permission to publish
the illustration of snowmen by her late husband Marko,
and to Chuck Grieve for publishing me and believing
in my work. The group Writers Abroad helped a great
deal with their comments. RARA in Cardiff gave me a
platform.

   This collection would not have been possible without
the support of my wife, Jill, and children, Naomi, Joe,
Chris and Kate.

– John Eliot, Cardiff, 2016

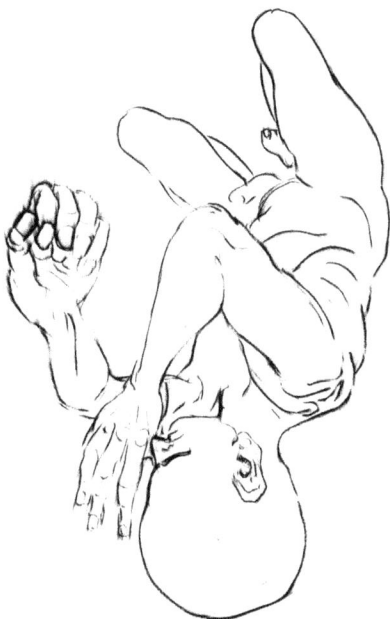

Please stay forever, I say to the things I know.
Don't go. Don't grow.

– Patti Smith

Love Song

I ate three soft peaches
for lunch, with cream. They
were overripe. I cannot remember
Prufrock's opening lines;
song of my youth, birth
of modern poetry.

People are dead to what
they will not understand.
Etherised.
I hear a reflection
calling my name:

If you are going to give me
immortality, why
refuse me? Because I
cannot but try
to overcome your piercing blue eyes
which make poets lyrical.

Door to bright silence:
the gap beneath
is death and birth.

Beach

Give me a place to stand
at the shore's edge;
pivot of a star.

I will see spirit red glow
of dawn sun;
cadaver slivered silver moon grey dusk.

Across the universe
I hear an echo held
in eternal silence.

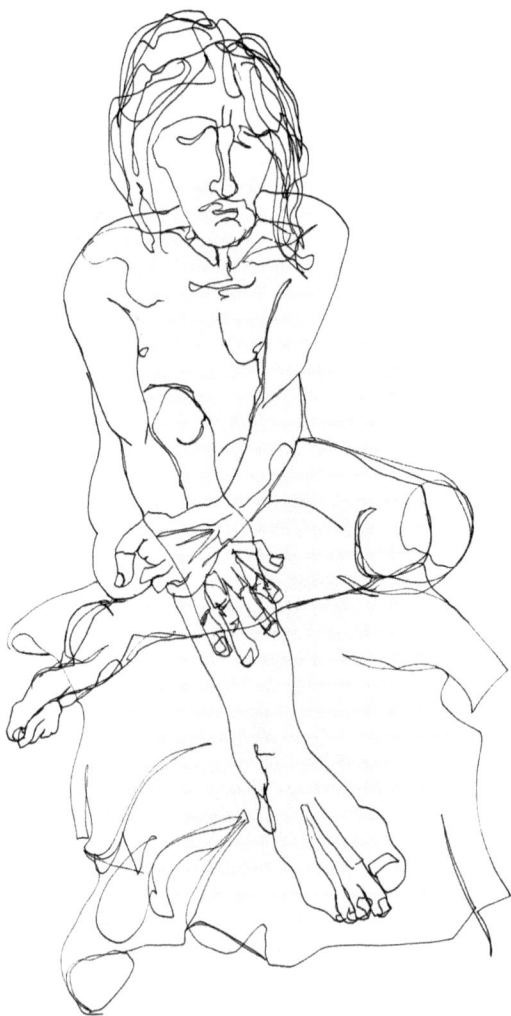

Prayer

I turn in my footsteps hearing
my protector still
keeping pace in disappearance
the depth
the chord
murmurs only
to me om

at the end of beginning
is light

I see blackness move
as a shade
across this red eternal desert
that some call heaven

Silence

A lone bird
fills the night.
Owl, screech.

Deep blackness, where I am,
four a.m.

Too soon silhouette of dawn.

Two plaintive cries,
then stillness.

Lying in bed,
seeing, not hearing peace.

My whisper is for
returning love:
sing me
to sleep.

Evening All Day

no sunset
no sunrise
no streaks of red
announce
a beginning
a dissolving

only a calotype
sepia silver crystal
sliding
against wire

suspended over
grey blue universe
called raindrop

Grey dawn

Stars shine
Deep yellow one by one
As moonlight fades
On tree-lined
Ditch-ragged lane

Who can say where we are going
Or where we have been
Blackness behind
Sienna darkness ahead

Climb until the faint line of sun snow
Reflects on hills of Merthyr
This winter day

Rhymney village hear
Early morning bells
Across the dying valley

See ghosts of miners
Smell smoke from chimneys
As they search for fires of home
This grey dawn

Dusk

dark spring
black light
thinness of the carped moon
wound seared raw
silhouetted against edge

hearing noise
deadwater moves
my gut turns
a coil
a wire
barbed hook tears a lip
plucks from the depths

Thorn

Blood on my hands,
berry-picking.
Gone is summer,
sounds of the child.

I stand
weary already of Autumn
watch the red drip
to brown earth

awaiting Winter
for another year
I ache.

For Carlton

A Winter Trilogy

I

21 December 2008

Break Fast in Belgium
Shortestday
Through pane
Wheels spin rain

735am
Piped carols ♫
In this Vilvoorde Motel
Hark The Herald Angels

Poised between
Plate & mouth
mirabile dictu
The mystery

Of how
Jesus liked his bacon

II

25 December 1958

Memory
A beaten path
To the past
Cold darkness
Before dawn

A moment's scent
Anticipation
The fire's blue glow
For a moment
As lights around
An artificial tree

We took the stairs
My sister and I
Each essential tread
How far away child Christmas

III

31 December 1983

5 4 3 2 1
A drunken man shouts

And people feign excitement

Another year

Shall we countdown to our death

An overfed bore
Approaches extending a hand
Woman
With florid face
Broken veins
Like vines
Pouts for a kiss

Frame of Words 4

A divorce!

But I love you.

No. You, don't.

In my poems. You can find my love for you.

Love of words.
You live in a box
rearranging alphabet
into order
that only you control.

Like a jazz player improvising, running
in parallel lines
with wayward bounce,
the listener pretends,
to understand.

So the artist draws lines,
creates as if a God,
Man and Woman
declare their love
for each other.

I'm trapped in a frame of words.
And from my brain grows
the flowering plant
named apple.

Framed

Carrying you
smiling man;
portrait
glass and frame.
A still fish.

Dropping you.
Shattering. Everything.
You writhe d about
grasping for eternity.
Picking you up,
pushing you,
behind the glass

there you stick
not, quite, right.
A blurred image
jumping in your blue
against white,
as the mask we wear.
Auto portrait.
Yes.

John 1

From the sky
hung a man.
In my glass I saw Him
reflected, outstretched,
cruciform wood. His face
the agony of life. And light
swept down from the heavens

before darkness
before beginning was made the end
before the Word.

Crucifix

Out of wood
a Biblical carpenter
works a cross
for the congregate
in cavernous spaces
genuflecting as their murmurs
sound within the building
invocating deity's death
forgetting the forest.

Humbled before the tree
I kiss the roots,
touch the wound of the axe,
where sap flows
to outstretched limbs;
leaves reaching
with promise of eternal life
after death of Man.

Sound of Glass

piano on the pain
a chord reccuring
repeating notes
repeating notes
repeating notes
hammer
chord chord chord

from my window
there is the
possibility of a rainbow

I stand still
hearing the colours
colours of the vowels
cauchemar to
find the finish

Beast

In the final moon
of last sunrise.
I stand alone
this grey dawn
at water's shore.
Beached breath,
but for final shriek
ahool and *cras*
the first raven.

A monster lies.
Silhouette against rising
still silence,
bare waste
branches move.

The beast, I can see,
but spectre of the deep,
I do not know,
I do not face.
This is my fate.

A Lullaby

Even at three and a half
I recognised
Brahms' Lullaby
as a song of death
hearing the minor key
playing at my funeral;

with my mother
in front of the old wooden wireless,
fixed up by my Father,
in the empty house
waiting for his return
I tried to love
the pathos.
She sought ways to pass time
with the foetus.
Unwanted mistake
uniquely created for abortion
never to see daylight,
a glow, sunrise,
red streaks, sunset,
white canvas to paint
pale yellow moon.

Her brain pitched
in turmoil
knowing only darkness,

grave blackness
buried in this earth.
As a flower,
she will not grow.

In Memory

Bradgate Moor where
Jane lay slain
grey ashes remain
still, lingering as the wind
blows on the empty hill.
Unmoving the spirit
of my Father

watches sun rise moon set
birth and death.
Beheaded trees
no branches to reach
green leaves, flowers sigh.
The spirit lingers still.

We climb these rocks
carrying death in an urn;
our burden. Scattering ashes;
Mother, in peace.

Footprints

Today is your birthday,
a few months since
we lit candles
leaving your ashes
congealed on the sodden hill.

Our anoraks
rejecting rain,
we pretended the occasion,
passed round a flask of coffee;
fizzy crisps.

To Mother, we shouted,
feebly singing into the wind
where, like yesterday's footprints,
our song was lost.

28th July 2015

Heol y Cyw

Did I expect to meet
Father walking the street
Man and Boy
crossing paths
looking for remains
on the earth

as I walk deserted avenues
searching for you

in a Cardiff square
listening to Mr Humphries
Morning has Broken
a favourite song

I knew you'd departed
this village long ago

and striking out
into the country
beneath an arch of trees
the falcon soared
leaving your Spirit to me

Photograph of the Dead Father

He pointed
to a thread-hung photograph;
strong young man,
handsome, playful smile; sparkle
in his eyes.

That was my Father:
a woman, children, loved him,
with pride he told us,
When his life
after the war began
in England. Before I was born.
Sighed,
He is gone now.

Again he looked at the face,
That was too long ago.

Deaf we were
to his thoughts.

I am dying. A year,
the doctors say.
Perhaps less or more.

Portrait from white, to grey, to black.
Death framed the dying man's wall.

Private Delver Hathway 1881-1915

Elysium dissolves
with the harvest of youth; August to September
summer mellows, and on an autumn day I lie as I die
in a chalk pit. I will not remember
September 28th 1915
death's moment; unholy joy, my heaven.

Hell is life stolen from the young.
Hell is those left behind.

Scorn for a ceramic poppy;
as my spirit marches these fields of Loos.

In memory of my great-uncle

i
around me are the living
hearing the screams
of the dead

living flesh;
bones of dry sticks,

never knowing peace,
unless
I am listening to the living,
rather than the dead.

ii
not that I dwell
in the land of the dead,
nor living.
but a purgatory.

iii
the beast, death
may not be feared

as it is
a candle alone,
flickering dying flame.
the death of rebirth.

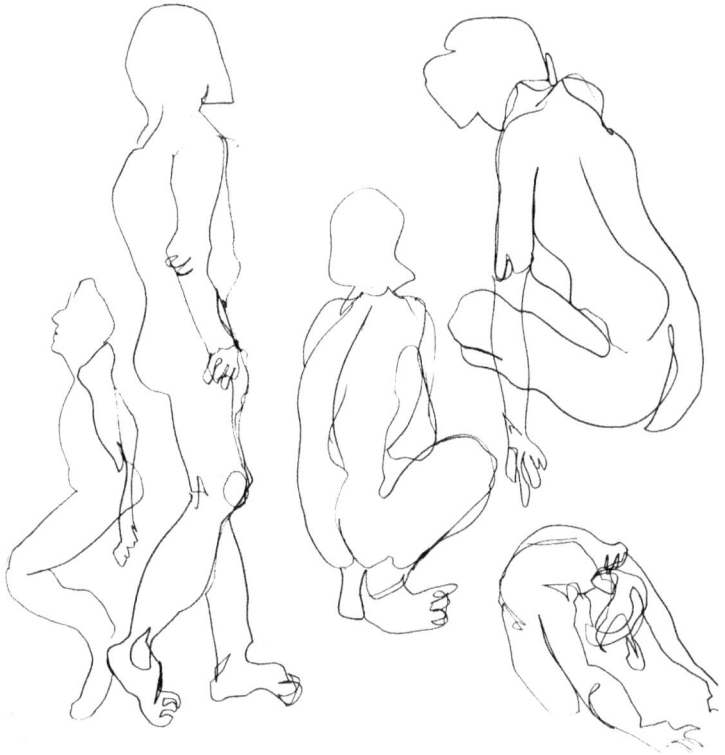

Snowmen

A dying friend gave me
his sketch
of snowmen.

Roughly hewn,
speedily drawn.
Flawless.

Six figures:
blue top hats, yellow scarves, orange noses,
stand against an eternity of white.

Fearfully they shout,
Don't throw us to the stars,
waiting the fate of the morning sun.

Go gentle into that sunrise.

In memory of Marko

Eating ice cream

A memory to grasp
like holding on
a cloud of pollen;
look at my fingers
and then it is gone.

Eating ice cream with Grandpa on Clifton Street.

A bench. We sat
as I ate my white cone.
I heard a lady say,
hauling a bag of shopping to her knee,
"You are mad,
taking blossom from a tree."

She wore a blue dress,
tight round the middle.

Earlier in the park, by the swings,
blowing dandelions
Grandpa and me.

"Watch. I'll tell you the time.
One o'clock, two o'clock. Then three.
Mummy will be home soon."

A memory to grasp
like holding on
a cloud of pollen;
look at my fingers
and then it is gone.

For Lilwen

Anne Jill

Two lovely women
Linger for a moment

Beneath a pear tree
Exchange a word

Above them
Vast sky blue

How is colour described
As I see it or you

Not knowing the intimacy
Beneath the pear tree

Teenage

Things always end before they start – Lou Reed

A singular memory
stays seated
on the bus.

The driver to our
right.

Did he watch the road,
or us,
as we clung
one last time

the journey
Dover to London.

I do not remember your name.
No memory of your face.
Only the tan of your legs
from the French summer sun,
forever remains.

Bois de la Cambre

As sunlight flickered
an illusion.
I saw her then;
or was that
my belief?

A memory,
through the ice-cream van window
hair caught across
her face.
But the distance was too great;
years.
As she turned,
she wasn't the girl
I'd loved
with the deep soul;
but another,
that few would find loving easy.

Shadows

St Katherine
keeps her light
locked inside
her mind

her cell
at night
she shines
for sailors on the sea

turning full circle
as sparkles reflect
upon the water

I
AWAKENING

Thunder sleeps
occasional grey clouds hang
this birth of day
pinpoint of stars
evaporate across sleepy villages
where human and animal
may wake
with hope
before creation
before sun's rays break the dream
before
the storm

II
BURIAL

Thin line
across the horizon
moonset dew morn
almost a rainbow

this day was made
for the Sun
break the dawn
mist weeping tears rising
with reverent anticipation
they wait
the sun
appears
across the stones
fully risen

and the people
move forward
as one shade
in celebration

III
IF

light in the sky
never returned
we sit at dawn waiting
glimmer of a line
across the horizon
for our sunbirth

Sound of Grass

I believed we'd been waiting
for the rain:
yellow parched
St Augustine grass.

I could hear stalks
swallow fresh water,
gift from the sky.

To the sound of grass
he was deaf, he said,
tuneless as an old gong.

We no longer
listen to the same song.
Understanding grass
and Philip Glass
is the sound of madness.

The moment was disturbed.
The magic broken,
love lost
and the rain ceased.

Anne Neville

Mourning in our separate silences
still in the Cathedral of Angers
I hear the spirit of Anne Neville
walking away from something
upon nothing.

On the sound of midnight
I stand at the church door
listening for your voice,
before the car crosses
empty expanses of countryside
to warmth, red flames
and the finding of hidden mists.

Thoughts of a Young Woman

St Mary and St Severus
watch over me;
lonely in this square
Cathedral majesty of silence?
I hear your voices,
St Severus and St Mary

wise and foolish Virgin,
who am I? Tomb of the bigamist
by his side wives lie.

Ring bells, Gloriosa,
Queen of toll;
I shout my reply,
None shall listen to my soul.

Taken, abandoned, desolate, in four walls;
alone with the crowd, named insane.
Hear me, where I stand,
as God would, a grain of sand.

Epitaph for an Artist

Twenty years since,
we sat drinking
red grape of the vine.
My health;
yours too.

French country garden,
wild, overgrown, hidden;
home of a relentless artist.
With wonder,
I breathed in paintings;
your very existence.

Last night, we sat again, santé.
Raised glasses,
Grandchildren, our rebirth.
Santé. One of us is dying.
Not me;
am I glad it is not to be.

My blood is red,
yours is brown.
Next Spring feeding flowers,
in a neat graveyard ground.

In memory of Ahmed

THE AUTHOR, John Eliot, was born in Leicester. He taught in the south-west of England before moving to France with his wife to write full-time. His first collection of poetry, *'Ssh,* was published by Mosaïque Press in 2014. His novel *The Good Doctor* was also published in 2014.

THE ILLUSTRATOR, Dave Daggers, has had several failed careers: photographer, body-painter, construction worker, writer, lecturer, film-maker, musician, steel-worker and TV presenter. He is currently trying to be a performance artist and illustrator. He often performs at the same venues as John Eliot but claims to be a better poet, a career he has not yet tried.

www.ingramcontent.com/pod-product-compliance
Lightning Source LLC
Chambersburg PA
CBHW071937020426
42331CB00010B/2913